DEAN'S WELCO

YOU ARE AMONG the nearly one million visitors each year wh to welcome to St George's Chapel, Windsor Castle. I hope guidebook will add to the enjoyment of your time here, and that a pleasing memento of an interesting and happy visit.

St George's Chapel is a wonderful building; it can make a powerful impression on people. At the same time, the rich combination of architecture, craftsmanship, heraldry and historical associations can be overwhelming. When this is the case, many of us find it helpful to have our attention drawn gently both to major features and intriguing details. This guidebook is designed to do just that.

Standing in the Chapel, we see the results of centuries of architectural and artistic achievement. We also experience a deep sense of this nation's history, and feel as if we come close to some of those who have most shaped it. People are often touched by its special atmosphere.

Of course, something else contributes to the quality of the atmosphere. It is the fact that St George's is a place of worship and that, from the start, God's praises have been said or sung here every day.

The Chapel is at the heart of a community of people who live and work in Windsor Castle. Our daily worship expresses a conviction that the pursuit of truth and genuine human wellbeing requires us to maintain a vision of God, and to acknowledge our dependence on God and our accountability to God.

This place, and all that goes on within it from day to day, could constitute a kind of invitation to be more thoughtful about life. A visit to St George's Chapel could well become an occasion on which you stand in silence for a while, think about things spiritual, say a prayer or join us at one of our services.

Whatever your personal response to St George's might be, I hope that you will feel somehow blessed and enriched by your visit.

The Dean of Windsor is also Register of the Order of the Garter. The badge of office depicts crossed quills set against the book in which the register is kept of the Knights of the Garter attending meetings and services, the whole surrounded by a Garter.

The South Front of St George's Chapel.

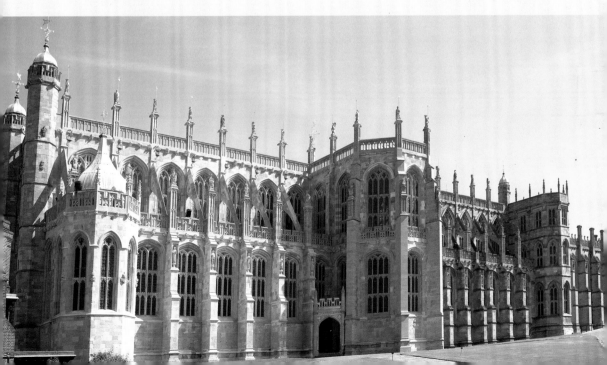

WORSHIP AND
A WELCOME TO VISITORS

S ERVICES ARE HELD in St George's Chapel every day of the year, and are open to all. These times of prayer, music, silence and readings follow a pattern through the week and through the Church year. The Chapel Choir sings regularly at about eight services each week during term time. The Choristers (boys between the ages of seven and thirteen) attend St George's School, situated immediately outside Windsor Castle.

St George's Chapel opens its doors to visitors whenever possible between services. Pilgrims and visitors have been welcomed to the Chapel since it was built. In the fifteenth and sixteenth century, many pilgrims came to visit the burial place of Henry VI. Although some considered the King to be ineffective, he was devout and regarded by many as a saint.

■ Holy Communion is celebrated at least once each day. Here the service is taking place in the Rutland Chantry.

His body was brought to Windsor in 1484. The pilgrims' alms box that stands beside the tomb dates to *c*.1480 and was made by John Tresilian. There are twenty slots for money and four different keys were required for simultaneous opening.

Pilgrims were also attracted to St George's Chapel by the presence of the Cross Gneth, represented, since its disappearance in the sixteenth century, by a ceiling boss at the south east end of the Chapel. The story is told that a priest named Neotus brought a piece of the Cross on which Jesus was crucified from the Holy Land to Wales, where it became a national treasure. The relic came into the hands of King Edward I in 1283 after Llewelyn, Prince of Wales, was killed in battle. The relic was given to the College of St George by King Edward III, soon after he founded the Order of the Garter in 1348.

■ Tomb of King Henry VI (reigned 1422 to 1461, and 1470 to 1471). Beside the tomb stands a pilgrims' alms box made by John Tresilian. The initial 'H' may be for Henry.

Today, visitors continue to make their way to St George's Chapel. Whether the visit is to offer prayer, to wonder at the architecture, to attend a service, to link the historic past with the present or simply to absorb the atmosphere, all are welcome. Prayers left by visitors during the day are offered at one of the services the following day.

Services take place throughout St George's Chapel – sometimes in the Quire, sometimes in the Nave or in one of the side chapels.

■ Boss depicting the Cross Gneth between the kneeling figures of Edward IV and Richard Beauchamp, Dean of Windsor and Bishop of Salisbury. A boss is a projecting ornament concealing the joints where the stone ribs of a vault meet.

Young visitors with a volunteer member of the Guild of Stewards.

■ Opposite: The Quire of St George's Chapel seen from the first-floor chantry chapel of Edward IV.

■ The Hastings Chantry in the North Quire Aisle was built towards the end of the 15th century in memory of William, Lord Hastings. The paintings depict the life and death of St Stephen, the first Christian martyr.

■ Right: The stoning of Stephen.

■ Above the door to the chantry in the South Quire Aisle is a rebus displaying Canon John Oxenbridge's name in picture form – an ox, a backwards facing 'N' and a bridge. Inside, the ceiling mirrors that of the Hastings Chantry, but the pictures depict the story of John the Baptist.

These small chapels were set up as chantries where masses were said daily for the souls of the departed. St George's was made exempt from the dissolution of chantries at the time of the reformation in 1547 but it is likely that daily masses for the dead ceased to be held in these small chapels soon afterwards. Today, they are frequently used for morning services.

ROYALTY FROM EARLIER TIMES TO THE PRESENT DAY

A CHURCH HAS STOOD within Windsor Castle for centuries; King Henry III dedicated one to Edward the Confessor on the site of what is now the Albert Memorial Chapel. The east wall of St George's Chapel bears witness to this earlier thirteenth-century building, with its squat arches and the doorway which was once the entrance to that other building.

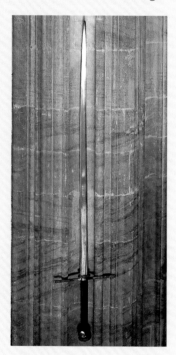

■ Above: The 13th-century doorway is sometimes used by the Sovereign and other members of the Royal Family.

■ Below: Details of the metalwork on the Gilebertus door.

■ This sword hung over Edward III's stall in the 13th-century Chapel. During the Commonwealth period it was hidden from the Cromwellian troops. 6' 8" (2 metres) long and made to be used to fight two-handed in battle, its use would have required training and practice from an early age.

■ Opposite: Edward III, founder of the Order of the Garter. He wears the crown of England and carries the crowns of Scotland and France skewered on his sword. This portrait was painted some 240 years after Edward's death in 1377.

Edward IV left very specific instructions in his will about his burial – he was to be buried below ground with a chantry chapel above.

Stained-glass portrait of King Henry VIII, situated in the South Quire Aisle.

The Nave of St George's Chapel.

The architectural story of St George's looks back, not as far as the thirteenth century, but to the two centuries that followed. In 1348, Edward III founded a new order of chivalry, 'The Order of the Garter'. It is the highest order of chivalry in the land and the oldest surviving in the world. Edward III, at war with France and possibly inspired by tales of Arthur and his Knights of the Round Table, resolved to form a band of distinguished soldiers to inspire loyalty, encourage military excellence and reflect the ideal manifestation of Christian chivalry. At the same time, the King founded the College of St George. The term 'College' was not used in the modern sense of an academic institution but to describe a group of clergy and laity who lived and worked together as a community. This remains the case today; members of the College live in the various cloisters and ensure that daily prayers are said for the Sovereign and the Companions of the Order of the Garter. The Dean and Canons of Windsor govern and are entirely responsible for the College, which, in a physical sense, takes up about a quarter of Windsor Castle.

Lay Clerks (the men of the choir) outside their homes in the Horseshoe Cloister.

Edward III's great-great-grandson, King Edward IV, decided to erect the present building as the Chapel of the Order of the Garter, and chose it as his eventual burial place. He was detailed in his will regarding the place of his burial and lies, with his wife Elizabeth Woodville at his side, in the north east corner of St George's. Before he died he would have seen the start of the building works, which began in 1475 and resulted in a spectacular example of perpendicular architecture. Large windows and slender pillars give an appearance of light and delicacy, while the pale colour of Taynton stone adds to the elegance of the structure. The fan vaulting, with its numerous bosses, and the frieze of stone

Opposite: Arms of Henry VIII above the organ loft, surrounded by the coats of arms of the Knights of the Garter of his time.

angels that lines the entire chapel draw the eyes upwards. Within 53 years the building was completed. By then, Henry VIII was King and his coat of arms, along with those of the Knights of the Garter of his time, can be seen directly above the organ loft. Henry VIII adapted the chantry chapel of Edward IV by adding a wooden oriel window in order that services in the Quire could be viewed by his first wife Catherine of Aragon. It is said that his sixth and last wife, Catherine Parr, watched his funeral service from the same vantage point. Henry VIII is buried in the centre of the Quire.

■ Opposite: Ledger stone in the centre of the Quire marking the burial spot of Henry VIII and Charles I.

After years of religious turmoil and the split from the Roman Catholic Church, different sovereigns embracing Catholic or Protestant views appointed Deans and Canons according to the beliefs in the ascendancy at the time. One man who survived a sentence of death despite his Calvinist beliefs was John Marbeck. He was a composer, Organist and Lay Clerk and lived, it is thought, in a fifteenth-century framed house to the north of the Chapel, in an area known as Denton's Commons. Marbeck had a remarkable escape, gaining a reprieve due to his musical ability. A few years later, Bishop Giles Tomson (Dean of Windsor and Bishop of Gloucester) was one of the translators of part of the New Testament. The result was what has become known as the 'King James' or 'Authorised' version of the Bible, published in 1611. Less than 40 years later, civil war broke out between Royalist and Parliamentarian factions in the country. St George's Chapel escaped the major damage that some other church buildings suffered during the war, and although the priests were thrown out of the Castle, some lay members of the College, the Poor or Alms Knights (now the Military Knights of Windsor), ensured the College's continuity. King Charles I was eventually put on trial, sentenced to death and beheaded. His body was brought to Windsor and, having lain overnight in the Castle, was carried to the Chapel for burial. Snow fell and turned the black pall covering the coffin to white. The interment was in the same vault used for Henry VIII. The date on the ledger stone commemorating Charles I might appear, at first glance, to be incorrect. The date '1648' was in accordance with the Julian calendar rather than the Gregorian one (which did not come into use in England until 1752). The Julian calendar held that the new year began on 25 March and the King's execution took place on 30 January – before the start of the new year. During the reign of King Charles II, Christopher Wren, son of a Dean of Windsor and architect of St Paul's Cathedral,

■ Bishop Tomson.

The Military Knights of Windsor after a service.

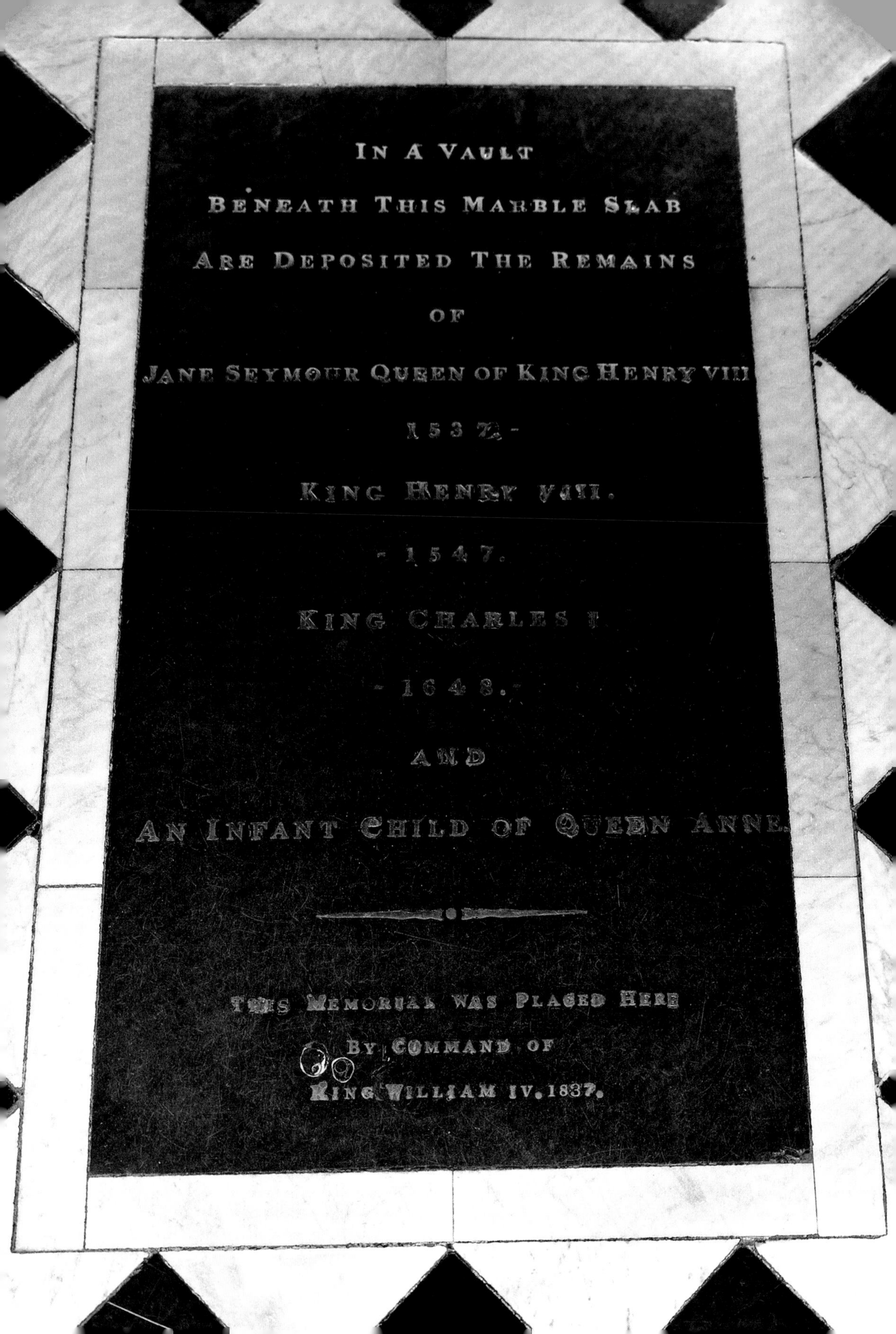

IN A VAULT

BENEATH THIS MARBLE SLAB

ARE DEPOSITED THE REMAINS

OF

JANE SEYMOUR QUEEN OF KING HENRY VIII

1537.

KING HENRY VIII.

1547.

KING CHARLES I.

1648.

AND

AN INFANT CHILD OF QUEEN ANNE.

———————•———————

THIS MEMORIAL WAS PLACED HERE

BY COMMAND OF

KING WILLIAM IV. 1837.

oversaw some refurbishment work in the Chapel.

A century after the restoration of the monarchy, King George III came to the throne. During his reign, several notable changes were made to St George's Chapel. Henry Emlyn designed a screen, made from Coade stone, to support a large new organ built by Samuel Green of Isleworth. Extra stalls (or seats) were added to the Quire, the carving of which, under the direction of Emlyn, blends almost seamlessly with the original. On close inspection, carved depictions showing scenes from the life of George III can be seen. Also, the words of Psalm 20 which run along the back of the centre row of stalls are interrupted by the words 'God Save the King' and 'God Bless the Prince'. George III also commissioned the royal vault to be excavated. He, his wife Queen Charlotte, his sons King George IV and King William IV, and other members of the royal family are interred there. George IV had a daughter, Princess Charlotte, who would have acceded to the throne had she survived. Her death, and that of her stillborn child, in 1817, is marked by a monument in the Urswick Chantry. Charlotte's cousin, Victoria, inherited the crown at the age of 18, after William IV's death. Widowed by the death of Prince Albert in 1861, Queen Victoria spent much of her time in Windsor and used the oriel

■ Far Left: Memorial to Princess Charlotte in the Urswick Chantry.

■ Left: King Leopold of the Belgians, husband of Princess Charlotte. His membership of the Order of the Garter is indicated by the Garter around his left leg, just visible below the knee.

window overlooking the high altar in the Quire to watch services – the same vantage point used by Catherine of Aragon some 350 years earlier. Today, the chantry chapel behind the oriel window is used weekly for services. The view that it affords down into the Quire means that the chapel is sometimes used for television cameras when major services are broadcast.

Victoria's son and heir, Edward, married Alexandra of Denmark in St George's Chapel. The tomb where they are buried, to the south of the high altar, brings together the regal and the personal through the sculpture of Caesar, King Edward VII's dog, shown lying at his master's feet.

In the 1920s, King George V and Queen Mary oversaw a major restoration of the Chapel. The tomb of George V and Mary depicts the King in the uniform of an Admiral of the Fleet and the robes of the Order of the Garter, and the Queen with her hands clasped in prayer in a uniquely personal manner. The effigies were sculpted by Sir William Reid Dick and placed on a base designed by Sir Edwin Lutyens.

◼ Tomb of George V and Queen Mary.

The Queen's procession departs from the West steps following the service on Garter Day.

King George VI, who reigned from 1936 to 1952, reinstated the annual service of thanksgiving for the Order of the Garter soon after the Second World War. Although the Order itself had remained firmly in place as the highest order of chivalry bestowed by the monarch, a service of thanksgiving, including installations, had fallen into disuse. The service, preceded by a procession from the State Apartments to St George's Chapel, now takes place each year in June.

Following King George VI's death, a new side chapel was built off the North Quire Aisle. It was designed by George Pace, with windows by John Piper. Today, the bodies of King George VI and Queen Elizabeth the Queen Mother are interred there, together with the ashes of The Princess Margaret. On the gates guarding the entrance are the words from a poem by Minnie Louise Haskins, used by the King in a radio broadcast on Christmas Day in 1939 – the first Christmas of the Second World War.

The Sovereign's stall is unique amongst the stalls in the Quire. Below the seat is an outstanding fifteenth-century misericord commemorating an occasion Edward IV was very proud of – the conclusion, between himself and King Louis XI of France, of the Treaty of Picquigny in 1475. Above the stall are the banner and crest of the Sovereign but, unlike any other stall, there are no stall plates; the continuity of sovereignty requires none as there is always a Sovereign of the Order of the Garter.

■ Opposite: The Sovereign's stall in the Quire with banner, crest, helm, mantling and sword.

'I said to the man who stood at the gate of the year, Give me a light that I may tread safely into the unknown And he replied Go out into the darkness and put your hand into the hand of GOD, that shall be to you better than a light and safer than a known way'

In 2005, Prince Charles, The Prince of
Wales, and The Duchess of Cornwall,
celebrated their marriage with a service
of dedication and prayer.

The Knights of the Garter presented
Queen Elizabeth II with an eightieth birthday
gift in 2006 – a bronze bust by the sculptor,
Angela Conner.

The service of dedication and
prayer following the marriage of
The Prince of Wales and The
Duchess of Cornwall was held in
St George's Chapel in April 2005.

■ Bronze portrait of Elizabeth II
presented in her 80th year.

CHAPEL, COMMUNITY AND BEYOND

ST GEORGE'S CHAPEL, though independent of the Royal Household, sits geographically within Windsor Castle. Primarily, it is a place of daily worship – it is the Chapel of the Order of the Garter and of the College of St George. It is also a place where visitors from far and wide are welcomed, where connections with many countries and institutions are celebrated and commemorated, and where many – both known by name and anonymous – have given of their time, their gifts and their money over the centuries. One of the most important benefactors in the early years of the Chapel was Sir Reginald Bray. Upon his death in 1503, he left a large legacy to the College of St George for the completion of St George's Chapel.

In more recent times, many have given gifts to help maintain the fabric of the Chapel and its surrounding buildings, to help ensure the continuance of the musical tradition at the Chapel and to the founding in 1966 of St George's House, a consultation centre. Each year in April, most of the new Queen's Scouts from throughout the United Kingdom gather at St George's for a service of celebration and thanksgiving. In 2007, the Scouts centenary year, the Scout Association's gift of new furniture for the Rutland Chantry was dedicated.

■ New furniture made by Luke Hughes in 2007 sits alongside the 16th-century tomb of Lord Roos and his wife, Anne Manners.

■ The badge of Sir Reginald Bray – a hemp brake used for crushing hemp – appears 175 times in glass, stone and metal throughout the Chapel. Shown here are two examples – the lock of the door to the Bray Chantry where he is buried, and a boss in the North Nave Aisle.

■ Stall Plate of Sir Walter Paveley.

One notable group of people who live within the Castle community, and who hold a unique place in the College of St George, are the Military Knights of Windsor. Founded in 1348 as part of the College, they were called Poor Knights, appointed to pray daily for the Knights of the Garter. The name changed in 1833 to the Military Knights of Windsor. Consisting of a Governor and twelve officers, they attend services on a weekly basis and, when able, contribute on a voluntary basis and in a variety of ways to the life of the Chapel. For many, Windsor Castle will be their last home, having spent a lifetime of service travelling, often overseas. Within and outside St George's Chapel, many previous Military Knights are honoured. Individuals with roots or connections overseas are also remembered, be they Knights of the Garter, those from foreign lands or Britons noted for their exploits abroad. One of the earliest stall plates in the Quire is that of Sir Walter Paveley who in 1346 and 1356 fought the French at Crecy and Poitiers. A more recent French connection is illustrated by the cenotaph of the Prince Imperial.

Connections with other countries range from the banners (hanging in the Quire) of various Scandinavian and Benelux Stranger Knights to the 2001 window in the Dean's Cloister commemorating the centenary of the Australian Federation.

St George's Chapel belongs to no diocese, and is not under any provincial or diocesan authority. It is, therefore, independent and able to be a focus of welcome and worship not only to those within the local community but also in the lives of many from countries across the world.

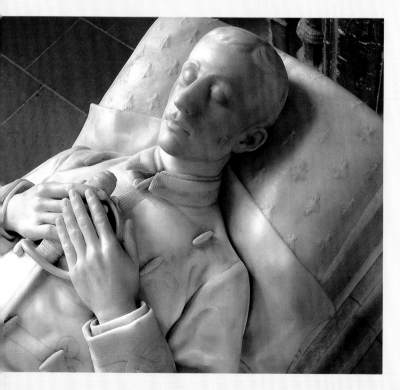

■ The Prince Imperial, son of Emperor Napoleon III of France, fled to England with his family in 1870 after the Emperor was deposed. He died in 1879 serving in the British Army in the Zulu war. He rests his head upon a pillow covered with bees, a symbol of the French Imperial family.

THE HON.BLE LIEUT. COL. HARCOURT WITH 30 DRAGOONS
OF THE 16TH REGT. TAKING THE AMERICAN GENERAL
LEE PRISONER ON THE 13TH OF DECR. 1776.

■ The Australia Window in the Dean's Cloister.

■ The coat of arms of Canada as depicted on the tomb of George V in the Nave.

■ Stall plate of Emperor Yoshihito of Japan.

■ Above: Detail of the plinth to the statue of the 3rd Earl Harcourt.

ARTISTRY AND CRAFTSMANSHIP

Stone carvings, known as grotesques, encircle the outside of the Chapel at two levels. A creature sits atop a downpipe near the south door and clutches a tiger or lion in its hands.

W HEREVER THE EYE LOOKS, inside or outside St George's Chapel, there is evidence of master craftsmanship, from its earliest fifteenth-century features to the modern touches that enhance the graceful and spectacular perpendicular architecture. Carving in wood and stone that is over 500 years old combines with work from the eighteenth century to the present day. At the start of the building work, Thomas Cancellor, William Berkeley, Henry Janyns and John Tresilian (Clerk of Works, Head Carver, Head Mason and Head Smith) came together under the leadership of Richard

Beauchamp, Bishop of Salisbury and later Dean of Windsor. One of the masons employed a little later, William Vertue, who completed the Nave and the Quire vaulting, may be the person depicted in the lower right hand light of the west window, mallet in hand.

The angel frieze that runs around the entire Chapel beneath the clerestory windows, as well as the vibrant grotesques outside, is testament to the skill of the masons and stone carvers – a skill that is still in demand in the twenty-first century.

■ A popey or poppy head at the end of a row of stalls in the Quire, carved during the 15th century, depicts the crucifixion.

The carving of new grotesques for St George's has encouraged a creative relationship between the staff and students of the City & Guilds Institute and the College of St George.

A 21st–century replacement for an earlier eroded grotesque of unknown design.

■ Opposite: Of the 75 principal lights in the west window, 65 date from before 1509. Banners designed and made by Thetis Blacker hang in the Nave on certain occasions.

Woodcarvers used their tools, skill and imagination to produce works ranging from religious scenes to purely humorous ones, and wooden busts for the helms of Knights of the Garter to rest upon.

The earliest stained glass dates from c.1500, much of it in the vast area of the west window, which measures 36 x 29 feet (11 metres x 9 metres). Elsewhere, heraldic glass and portraits of sovereigns and consorts are complemented by the 1960s work of John Piper in the George VI Chapel. The gates outside this small chapel in the

North Quire Aisle were designed by George Pace to reflect the style of the work of the Cornishman, John Tresilian, considered to be the finest metalworker of the Middle Ages. The wrought iron gates, both magnificent and delicate, were made for the tomb of Edward IV.

■ Above: Arm rests in the stalls of the Lay Clerks.

■ Left: Beneath each helm of the current Knights of the Garter sits a different wooden bust. Carved during the late 15th century, each one has long features, designed to be seen from below, and shows the head and shoulders of a man wearing a blue garter mantle fastened by a cord over a white under-vestment and a brown surcoat laced at the throat.

■ Opposite: The work of John Tresilian, seen here in a detail of the gates made to guard the tomb of Edward IV, is both delicate and detailed.

■ Opposite: Adoration of the Magi is one of five embroidered hangings made by Beryl Dean between 1969 and 1974. Originally hung in the Rutland Chantry, they are now housed in a cabinet to protect them from light and dust, although at least one is on display at any one time.

Some of the door locks that Tresilian made are still in use after 500 years.

Other forms of artistry abound within the Chapel. Modern embroidery and fabrics change with the liturgical seasons and new stall plates echo earlier ones. Exhibitions of art are held on a regular basis in the Dean's Cloister and music enhances some acts of worship six days a week during term time. The music sung and played ranges from that of the earliest days of plainsong to pieces specially commissioned for St George's by composers such as Benjamin Britten, William Harris and Peter Maxwell Davies.

■ This surrounding for a latchpull can be seen on the door leading up to the chantry chapel above Edward IV's tomb.

Music from many centuries is played and sung in St George's Chapel.

■ 20th-century icon depicting the Annunciation.

HERALDRY
AND THE ORDER OF
THE GARTER

■ Stall Plate of The Prince of Wales.

E DWARD III FOUNDED the Order of the Garter in 1348. Originally, Companions of the Order (as Knights of the Garter are sometimes known) consisted of the Sovereign, The Prince of Wales and 24 members. Since those early days, two other categories have swelled the numbers. They are Stranger Knights, who are Sovereigns of other countries, and members of the British Royal family other than the Sovereign and The Prince of Wales.

Knights were drawn, at the Order's foundation, exclusively from the fighting nobility close to the King. Today, distinguished former service personnel are sometimes made Knights of the Garter but other walks of life, such as business, exploration, law and politics are also represented.

The vaulting of the Nave, completed in 1506, is covered in bosses showing the heraldic arms or badges of Knights of the Garter from the late fifteenth

■ Stall Plate of Tsar Alexander II of Russia.

■ Stall plate of Sir Winston Churchill.

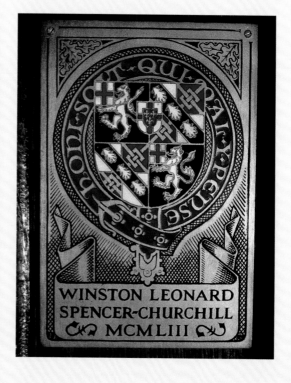

and early sixteenth century. Stained glass shows off the brilliant colours and sharp designs of heraldry. However, it is in the main body of the Quire that one of the best displays of heraldic art in the world can be seen. A banner hangs high above the stall of each of the current Knights of the Garter. Some designs have been passed down over many generations and may reach back to the times when it was essential to recognise the shapes and patterns on shields and clothing over armour, to distinguish friend from foe on the battlefield. Others are new and have been granted in recent times. Below each banner is a crest on top of a helm. Many crests, and sometimes the overall coat of arms, make use of a visual pun or a play on words. Lord Butler of Brockwell's crest is a badger atop a well and Sir Edmund Hillary's is a kiwi wielding an ice pick. In heraldic terms, the design on a banner is unique to an individual and can be inherited only by the heir. Coats of arms displayed by other members of the family must be changed or 'differenced' in some way with a small device such as a crescent or star, a martlet (small bird) or, in the case of the eldest son, by a 'label' (a white band with three points running across the width of the shield). Ladies of the Order have no crest or helm, reflecting the earlier days of the

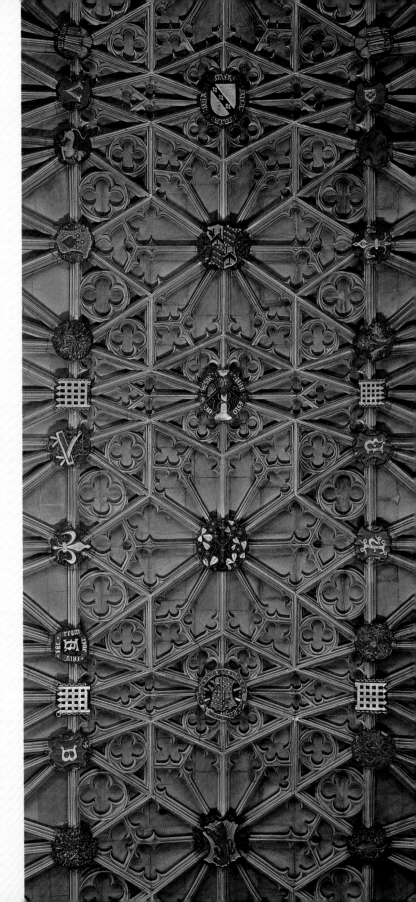

■ Nave vaulting, where bosses are decorated with religious symbols and heraldic devices of early Knights of the Garter.

■ Opposite: group of stall plates, ranging in date from 1392 to 1812.

■ Sir Edmund Hillary's crest and helm flanked by those of Lord Ashburton (left) and Sir Antony Acland.

Order when women did not play any military role. A half-drawn sword below the helm indicates the readiness of each male Companion to defend his Sovereign and religion. At the back of each stall (or seat) is a stall plate. Unlike the banner, crest, helm and sword, the stall plate remains in place after a Companion's death. As a result, of the approximately 1,000 Knights of the Garter that there have been since 1348, well over 700 stall plates remain. The rest have either been lost or deliberately removed.

Once a year, the Knights of the Garter process through the Castle and gather in their Chapel to attend a service of thanksgiving. This is just one example of the worship and service that is offered against the spectacular backdrop of richly carved woodwork and colourful heraldry.

■ Stall plate of the Duke of Norfolk, executed for treason in 1572. His stall plate was removed but returned to the Chapel in the 1950s, when it was placed on the rear of the stalls. It can be seen in the South Quire Aisle.

ST GEORGE

S T GEORGE REPRESENTS courage and fidelity linked with Christian chivalry and gentleness. He supplanted Edward the Confessor as patron saint of England, a process that took some 200 years and culminated in the elevation of his feast day to the same level of celebration as other major saints' days. This followed his supposed appearance over the battlefield of Agincourt in 1415.

The saint is depicted in various forms and materials at St George's Chapel and reminds all those that pass by that the qualities of love and care for humanity, courage in the face of adversity and a sense of what is true and right should remain at the forefront of daily life.

■ St George as depicted on the font at the west end of the Chapel.

■ Coade stone boss below the organ screen.

■ Opposite: Fountain in the Dean's Cloister, made in 1998 to mark the 650th anniversary of the College of St George. The figure is a copy of a 15th-century wooden carving originally from the Quire but now housed in the College's Archives.

Angel Frieze

Front cover
Quire view from the Organ loft

Back cover
South Nave Aisle

For further information
(including times of services)
please see our website
www.stgeorges-windsor.org
or ring our recorded information
line 01753 865 538

First published in 2008 by
Scala Publishers Ltd
Northburgh House
10 Northburgh Street
London EC1V 0AT
www.scalapublishers.com

ISBN 978 1 85759 537 6

10 9 8 7 6 5 4 3 2 1

Editor: Sandra Pisano
Designer: Nigel Soper
Printed in Singapore